W9-DDY-391

J 917.3 F799K
Fradin, Dennis B.
Kansas in words and pictures

M

Southwest Public Libraries
Grove City
91   3359 Park St.
Grove City, OH 43123

107

KANSAS

in words and pictures

BY DENNIS B. FRADIN

ILLUSTRATIONS BY RICHARD WAHL

MAPS BY LEN W. MEENTS

Consultant
Evangeline Thomas, CSJ, Ph.D.
President, Kansas Historical Society

COLUMBUS METROPOLITAN LIBRARY

 CHILDRENS PRESS, CHICAGO

Dedication: For My Wife, Judith

For their help, the author thanks:
Tom A. Witty, State Archeologist
Jim Marlett, Zoologist, Sedgwick County Zoo
The Pratt County Extension Office
Game Division of the Kansas Fish and Game Commission

Kansas Prairie

Library of Congress Cataloging in Publication Data

Fradin, Dennis B
  Kansas in words and pictures.

  SUMMARY: A history and description of the
Sunflower State.
  1. Kansas—Social conditions—Juvenile
literature. 2. Kansas—Economic conditions—
Juvenile literature. [1. Kansas] I. Wahl,
Richard, 1939- II. Title.
HN79.K2K7   978.1   80-12576
ISBN 0-516-03916-4

Copyright© 1980 by Regensteiner Publishing Enterprises, Inc.
All rights reserved. Published simultaneously in Canada.
Printed in the United States of America.

8 9 10 11 R 93 92 91 90 89 88

Picture Acknowledgments:
KANSAS DEPARTMENT OF ECONOMIC DEVELOPMENT—cover, 4, 11
(top and bottom), 19, 21, 24 (right), 25, 26, 29, 31, 32, 34 (bottom right),
35 (right), 36, 37, 38, 39, 40, 41, 42
JAMES P. ROWAN—2, 11 (center, left and right), 12
SALINA AREA CHAMBER OF COMMERCE—23, 28, 33 (left)
WICHITA'S HISTORIC COWTOWN—13, 14, 33 (right), 34 (left)
WICHITA AREA CHAMBER OF COMMERCE—34 (top right)
AGRICULTURAL HALL OF FAME—24 (left)
SEDGWICK COUNTY ZOO—35 (left)
COVER PHOTOGRAPH—Castle Rock

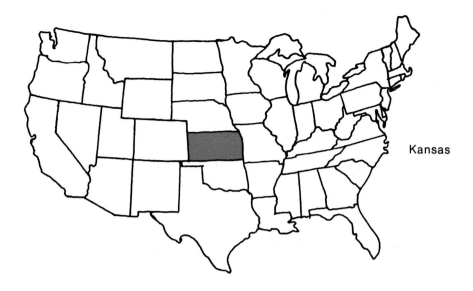

Kansas

Kansas was named after the Kansa Indians who once roamed the land. *Kansa* means "people of the south wind." The exact center of the United States is in Kansas—if you don't count Alaska and Hawaii. The center is near the town of Lebanon.

Kansas has long stretches of flat land and gentle hills. Much of Kansas is great for farming. Kansas is the leading wheat-growing state.

Kansas is also a leading cattle-raising state. Once, cowboys on horseback drove cattle to Dodge City and other Kansas towns. Wyatt Earp (WHY • ett ERP) and Bat Masterson were Kansas lawmen in those days. Modern cowboys herd cattle with jeeps and motorcycles.

Beech Aircraft Corporation in Wichita

Kansas has much more than wheat and cattle. Do you know where most private airplanes in America are made? Do you know where our 34th president, Dwight D. Eisenhower (DWHITE D. EYE • zen • how • er), grew up? Do you know where the famous flier, Amelia Earhart (ah • MEAL • yah AIR • hart), was born? As you will learn, the answer to all these questions is the Sunflower State, Kansas.

About 100 million years ago there were huge flying dinosaurs in Kansas. One fossil found near the Smoky Hill River had a wing span of 25 feet. It was as big as a small airplane.

Fossils of sea turtles and sharks have been found in Kansas fields. Crocodile bones have been found. They prove that, millions of years ago, the land was covered by water.

The ancient oceans dried. About a million years ago, the weather turned very cold. The Ice Age began. Huge sheets of ice, called *glaciers* (GLAY • shurz), moved slowly over northeastern Kansas. The glaciers smoothed the land. They also ground up rocks into good, rich soil.

People came to Kansas at least 10,000 years ago. Their stone tools, pottery, and burial mounds have been found. The earliest people tracked buffalo herds. They also hunted *mammoths*, which looked like big hairy elephants. Later people learned to farm. Farming meant they could live in one place. They built villages, remains of which can be seen today.

The Indians may be related to some of the ancient people. Many Indian tribes made their homes in Kansas. During the 1500s there were four main tribes. They were the Kansa (also known as Kaw), Pawnee (paw • NEE), Osage (OH • sayj), and Wichita (WITCH • eh • taw).

The Indians farmed and hunted. In the spring they planted corn, beans, and pumpkins. Then most of the summer they hunted. At one time, millions of buffalo grazed on the Kansas plains. Indians killed buffalo and deer with spears or bows and arrows. The meat was food. Deerskin was used to make clothes. Buffalo skins were used to make *tepees,* or tents. In the fall, the Indians returned to harvest their crops. They held feasts—with dancing, songs, and sports. Then they went on the fall hunt. This hunt lasted until snow covered the land.

The Pawnee lived in *earthlodges.* These were log houses covered by dirt.

Sometimes 40 friends and relatives lived in one earthlodge. Grandmothers looked after the children.

The Spanish were the first explorers in Kansas. Spain controlled Mexico, far south of Kansas. They wanted gold. They heard tales of a city of gold named *Quivera* (kwe • VAIR • ah). The streets were said to be made of gold. The houses were made of jewels. In 1541 the Spanish explorer Coronado (kor • oh • NOD • oh) went, with 300 soldiers, to find the city of gold. Indian guides led them northward. They came to what is now Kansas. The city of *Quivera* turned out to be a Wichita Indian village. It had grass huts instead of jeweled houses.

Spain claimed Kansas. But Spain lost interest in Kansas because no gold was found there.

France then claimed Kansas. During the 1600s and 1700s, a few French explorers and hunters arrived. Fur traders came, too. They traded pots, beads, and mirrors to the Indians. In return they received animal furs. Furs could be made into fancy hats and fine clothes.

In 1776 a new country was formed in America—the United States of America. The Americans had to fight and win the Revolutionary War to form their country. In 1803 the young United States bought a huge piece of

land from France. This was called the Louisiana Purchase. In this way most of what is now Kansas passed into the hands of the United States.

Kansas wasn't a state yet. It was land owned by the United States. President Jefferson sent Meriwether Lewis (mar • ih • weather LOO • iss) and William Clark to explore. In 1804 Lewis and Clark camped at the mouth of the Kansas River. They made maps and described the land. In 1806 the American Captain Zebulon (ZEB • yoo • lon) M. Pike explored Kansas. He called it a "sandy desert." Other explorers thought that crops wouldn't grow in Kansas.

In the Eastern United States, white settlers were taking Indians' lands. The United States looked for a place to send Indians. Many were sent to the "Great American Desert." The Delaware, Kickapoo, Iowa, and Chippewa (CHIP • ah • wah) Indians were moved to reservations in Kansas starting in about 1825.

For many years, white Americans only passed through Kansas. They were headed for other places. In 1821 the Santa Fe Trail was built through Kansas. Traders on mules rode through Kansas on their way to Santa Fe, New Mexico. In 1827, the first permanent United States settlement was formed in Kansas. It was Fort Leavenworth. Soldiers from the fort guarded travelers. Fort Larned and Fort Riley were also built in Kansas to protect travelers on trails.

By the thousands, people passed through Kansas. They traveled in covered wagons. Some were on their way to the California gold fields.

Fort Larned (above) was built by the U.S. Army in 1859. Fort Riley (left) was the base of operations for handling Indian uprisings. It is now the home of the 1st Infantry Division.

Much of the land in Kansas is great for farming.

Some people looked closely at Kansas soil. "It's not a desert after all," they said. "Kansas has good farmland." They decided to stay and live there.

Up to this time Kansas had been reserved for the Indians. In 1854 the Territory of Kansas was formed. Now Kansas was opened for settlement by white Americans. Many Indians were driven out. They were sent to Oklahoma.

Munger House, in Cowtown, was built in 1869.

Settlers poured into Kansas. Between 1855 and 1860 the population grew from about 8,600 to about 107,200. People came in groups of wagons called "wagon trains." Disease and Indian arrowheads kept some from reaching Kansas. Life was hard for those who got there. Where there were trees, the pioneers built wooden houses. But there were places where no trees stood as far as the eye could see. Some settlers cut up chunks of the hard ground—called *sod*—into brick-sized pieces. By piling up these bricks, they built warm sod houses.

The tough ground was good for building houses. But it made it hard to plant crops. Farmers hitched their oxen to plows and broke up the sod. Then grandparents, parents, and children planted corn seeds. The people watched the skies and hoped for rain. Farmers soon began to grow squashes, cucumbers, and tomatoes. They kept cows for milk and chickens for eggs.

When new settlers arrived, old ones helped them build their house. This was called a "house-raising."

Wichita's Cowtown has many restored buildings. The General Store (above) was built about 1884. It sold everything from shoes to bacon. The Red Schoolhouse (left) is a small one-room building, built about 1900.

Afterwards they had dancing and singing. Where many people lived in an area, schoolhouses were built. Churches and stores went up. Soon there was a town. Lawrence, Leavenworth, Atchison (AT • chih • son), and Topeka (ta • PEE • ka) were four towns founded in the 1850s.

Throughout the 1850s, people in the United States argued about slavery. In the South, black people worked as slaves. In the North, slavery wasn't allowed. Kansas was getting enough people to become a state. It wasn't in the North. It wasn't in the South. It was in the middle of the United States. Would it be a Free State with no slavery? Or would it be a Slave State? The Territory of Kansas as well as the Territory of Nebraska (neh • BRASS • kah) had been formed by the Kansas-Nebraska Act. This allowed the people in each territory to decide whether or not they would have slavery.

Some Kansans wanted a Free State. Others wanted Kansas to be a Slave State. Many people from outside Kansas came there to battle over slavery. On May 21, 1856, some Slave State people burned part of the town of Lawrence. John Brown, who battled against slavery for most of his life, then killed five Slave State men at Pottawatomie (pot • ah • WAH • tah • me) Creek. During this time there was so much fighting in Kansas that newspapers called it "Bleeding Kansas." In all, about 55 people were killed.

By the late 1850s, most Kansans were against slavery. The Free State people took control of the Kansas government. Slavery was banned in Kansas.

On January 29, 1861, Kansas became our 34th state. The capital was made at Topeka.

Kansas had been a state for only ten weeks when the Civil War began on April 12, 1861. The Civil War was fought between the Northern and the Southern states. Slavery was a big issue. Southern people were afraid they would have to give up slavery. Kansans had already battled over slavery. A Free State, Kansas sided with the North. Kansas sent a bigger percentage of soldiers to the Northern Army than any other state.

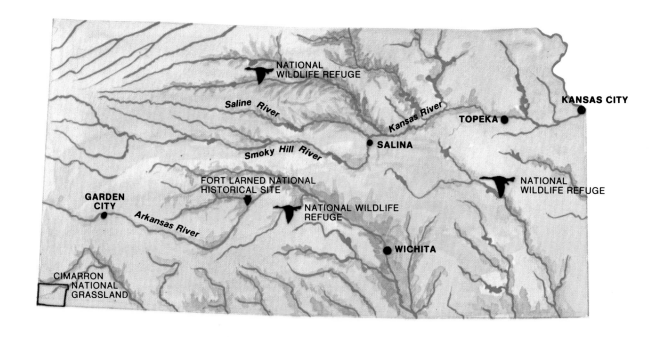

There were no major Civil War battles inside Kansas.
However, William C. Quantrill (quaun • TRIL), fighting
for the South, led raids into Kansas. At Lawrence—
already the scene of much violence—150 people were
killed.

The North won the Civil War in 1865. The United
States wanted more people to move westward to places
like Kansas. By the Homestead Act, people got land free
or very cheaply. Soldiers moved to Kansas. Freed slaves
came, too. People from around the world arrived.

Sunflowers

The pioneers saw zillions of sunflowers growing on the Kansas plains. People soon began calling Kansas the *Sunflower State*. Sunflowers move their heads from east to west following the sun across the sky. In this same way thousands of people were drawn West by the good land in Kansas!

In the late 1860s railroads were built into Kansas. It was easier to travel by train than by covered wagon. This helped even more families make Kansas their home.

The railroads also helped the cattle business. Two main trails—the Chisholm (CHIZ • um) and the Western—led to Kansas. Cowboys on horseback drove cattle herds all the way from Texas to Kansas. During the cattle drive, the animals ate the prairie grasses. Once in the Kansas "cow towns," the cattle were sent by train to markets in the East. Abilene (AB • ih • leen), Wichita, Ellsworth, Dodge City, and Caldwell were some of the Kansas cow towns. From about 1875 to 1885 Dodge City was the biggest cattle market in the world. It became known as the *Cowboy Capital of the World.*

During this time, there were many famous lawmen in Kansas. Bat Masterson was a famous gunfighter who

In 1955 the buffalo was named the state animal.

became a Dodge City lawman. Wyatt Earp worked as a lawman in Dodge City and Wichita. "Wild Bill" Hickok (HIK • ock) was a marshal of Hays City and Abilene. Tom Smith served as head lawman of Abilene. Smith used his fists instead of his gun to keep the law.

The face of Kansas changed greatly in the 1870s and 1880s. Buffalo provided food for railroad builders. One hunter, "Buffalo Bill" Cody, was said to have killed 4,280 buffalo in a year and a half. People also wore buffalo skin clothes. By 1880 the buffalo were almost wiped out.

The Indians were being driven out, too. Some Indians fought, but they had no chance against the United States Army. In 1867 many Indian tribes were forced to give up their Kansas lands. Buffalo Chief, a Cheyenne (SHY • an) Indian, said: "You give us presents and then take our land." Indian fighting ended in Kansas by 1878. Most of the Indians were pushed into Oklahoma. At one time over 30,000 Indians lived in Kansas. Today, there are only about 8,000.

Farmers wanted that fine Kansas land. Small farmers fenced in the ranges. By 1885, the cattle drives *to* Kansas were nearing an end. Farmers had fenced in the

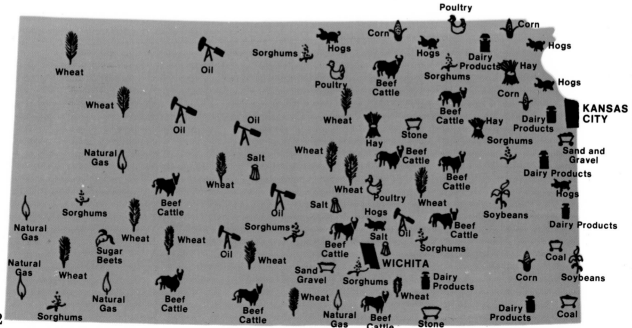

A Kansas
wheat field

ranges where the cattle grazed. Some ranchers began to raise cattle *in* Kansas.

Corn had always been the main crop in Kansas. A religious group called the Mennonites brought a kind of wheat known as Turkey Red to Kansas in 1874. Farmers found that the soil, rainfall, and climate of Kansas were perfect for growing wheat.

By World War I (1914-1918) Kansas was the *leading* wheat-growing state. The United States Army—and the rest of the country—ate bread made out of Kansas wheat. The state earned a new nickname: the *Breadbasket of America.*

Years ago farmers used steam-powered machines (left). Now they use faster, more modern machines like the combine (above).

Over the years, the farmers had many problems. Some years there were grasshoppers. Like a great black cloud, millions of grasshoppers filled the sky. They landed on crops and ate everything. Other years there were *droughts* (DROUTS). These were times of little or no rain. Crops withered and died.

Farming became a science in the 1900s. Kansas farmers started using machines. Machines helped them plant seeds. Machines helped them harvest crops. Better seeds were developed to grow bigger and better crops. Irrigation (bringing water to dry areas) was started. Today, water is stored in man-made lakes. Crops get the water from big sprinklers.

In the early 1900s, mining became important to Kansas. Oil wells were drilled in many places. Today Kansas is one of the ten leading oil-producing states. Natural gas—used to heat homes and fuel stoves—was also found. The biggest natural gas field in the world is near Hugoton.

Did you ever see a helium balloon rise to the sky? Helium is found in natural gas. It is used in rockets. The biggest helium factory in the world was built near the town of Liberal. Oil, natural gas, and helium have helped Kansas become a leading mining state.

An oil well in western Kansas

Ike's home in Abilene

In 1952, a Kansas man made history. His name was Dwight David Eisenhower. "Ike" was born in Denison, Texas. But when he was only two years old he moved to Abilene, Kansas. Eisenhower was commander of United States forces during World War II. From 1953-1961 Eisenhower served as our 34th president.

While Eisenhower was president, a black girl in Topeka named Linda Brown also made history. She wanted to go to an all-white school five blocks from her home. This wasn't allowed. At the time, most schools in U.S. cities were *segregated.* White students went to one school. Blacks went to another. Her father, Oliver Brown, brought the case to court. This important case— *Brown versus the Board of Education of Topeka*—went to the United States Supreme Court. In 1954 the Supreme Court ruled that it was against the law for schools to be segregated. Thanks to this case, black and white students go to school together in many U.S. cities today.

Above: Westinghouse Electric Corporation in Salina
Right: Working on a Beech airplane.

Today, many people still think of Kansas as only a
wheat-farming state. But more Kansans work in
factories than on farms. Many items are manufactured in
the state. Wichita produces most of the small airplanes
flown in America. Train cars and farm machines are also
made in Kansas. Cattle raised on Kansas ranches are
turned into meat in such cities as Wichita, Emporia (em •
PORE • e • ah), and Dodge City.

You have learned about some of the history of Kansas.
Now it is time for a trip—in words and pictures—
through the Sunflower State.

Kansas City, Kansas

On a map, you can see that Kansas looks much like a big rectangle. It isn't an exact rectangle. The Missouri River makes a squiggle in the northeast border.

From an airplane, you can see that Kansas has mostly flat land. Such flat land is called a *plain*. From the air, Kansas looks like a colorful patchwork quilt. There are blue lakes and rivers. The wheat fields are golden. Fields of corn and soybeans are green and yellow. There are red barns and white farmhouses.

You have arrived in a city by the Kansas River. This is Kansas City, Kansas. It is just west of Kansas City, Missouri.

Long ago, Kansa Indians lived in this area. Later, Wyandot (WHY • en • dot) Indians moved here. The Wyandot built a town and called it Wyandotte City. In this town, Wyandot Indians built the first public school in Kansas. Later, white settlers arrived. The town was renamed Kansas City.

Throughout its history, people and products have entered the state at Kansas City. That is why it is nicknamed the *Gateway to Kansas*. Today, Kansas City is the state's second biggest city. Meat is packed there. Wheat is stored there. Cars and soap are two other products. You can see how the soap is made. But they won't make you take a bath with it.

The oldest city in the state is just 30 miles northwest of Kansas City. This is Leavenworth. You can visit the

The University of Kansas

army post—Fort Leavenworth—that was built in 1827.
Leavenworth is famous for a place where you wouldn't
want to live—Leavenworth Prison.

About 35 miles southwest of Leavenworth is the city
of Lawrence. Lawrence is a center for education. The
University of Kansas is in Lawrence. A college for
Indians—Haskell Indian Junior College— is also there.

Topeka—the capital of Kansas—is just 27 miles west
of Lawrence. Long ago, many Indian tribes built their
villages by the Kansas River, where Topeka now stands.
The town was founded in 1854. Today, Topeka is the
state's third biggest city.

Above: John Steuart Curry's mural showing the settlement of
Kansas, in the State Capitol Building
Left: *Keeper of the Plains,* a sculpture created by an Indian,
Blackbear F. Bosin

Visit the State Capitol Building. Kansas lawmakers
meet there. The State Capitol Building is beautiful.
Many huge paintings by Kansas artists John Steuart
Curry and Lumen Martin Winter tell the story of the
state. You can see paintings of Coronado, John Brown,
Kansas farm families, and tornadoes.

Just one block from the State Capitol Building visit
the Kansas State Historical Society and Museum. At this
museum you can learn about people who lived in Kansas
10,000 years ago.

Above: Visitors in Cowtown
Left: The State Capitol Building in Topeka

Topeka has mills that turn Kansas wheat into flour. A famous railroad also has its headquarters in Topeka. It is the Atchison, Topeka, and Santa Fe.

The state's biggest city, Wichita, is about 138 miles southwest of Topeka. Once, Wichita Indians built their lodges here. The town was founded in 1870. In the 1870s cowboys drove cattle on the Chisholm Trail to Wichita. Later, oil found in the area helped Wichita grow into Kansas's biggest city.

Visit the Mid-America All-Indian Center in Wichita. There you can see arts and crafts from many Indian tribes. Nearby is the sculpture called *Keeper of the Plains*. It shows an Indian warrior.

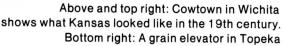
Above and top right: Cowtown in Wichita shows what Kansas looked like in the 19th century. Bottom right: A grain elevator in Topeka

Today, Wichita is a bright modern city with modern buildings. Wichita is known as the *Air Capital of the World*. Most small airplanes you see overhead were made in Wichita.

Wichita is the main manufacturing center in Kansas. Farmers send their wheat to Wichita, where it is ground into flour. Cattlemen send their cattle to Wichita stockyards. In Wichita the cattle quickly become meat.

Left: Sedgwick County Zoo, one of the best zoos
in America
Above: Century II in Wichita

One large building in downtown Wichita is shaped like
a flying saucer. It is called Century II. You can see plays
and hear fine music at this center. The Wichita Art
Museum has famous American paintings.

From Wichita, head west towards Dodge City. On the
way, you'll enter the heart of Kansas. North, south, east,
and west—almost everywhere you look you'll see wheat.

The wheat is planted in the fall. It begins growing in
the fall. All winter, it is covered by a blanket of snow.
Then in the spring and summer, the wheat grows higher.
By summer it is harvest time.

Farmers send their wheat to be stored in big buildings called grain elevators. The city of Hutchinson has one of the biggest grain elevators in the world. It is half a mile long. It can hold enough wheat to make a mountain of bread!

As you get nearer to Dodge City you'll also pass many cattle ranches. There are over six million beef cattle in Kansas. Cowboys still take care of the cattle. They brand them. Some ride jeeps or even motorcycles as they tend the herds.

About 153 miles west of Wichita you'll come to one of the most famous cowboy towns in America. This is

Cattle ready to be trucked to market

Front Street looks much the same as when Wyatt Earp and Bat Masterson lived in Dodge City.

Dodge City. Today, cowboys take cattle to Dodge City in trucks.

Dodge City is a small modern town. You may have seen movies and T.V. shows about the old "Wild West" days of Dodge City.

To relive those days, visit Boot Hill and Historic Old Front Street in Dodge City. Boot Hill was where cowboys were buried "with their boots on." Front Street has been rebuilt to look as it did in 1872.

Today, buffalo herds are kept in parks near Dodge City and elsewhere. Many other animals live in Kansas. There are deer. Coyotes howl on the Kansas plains. Prairie dogs dig their tunnels. Rattlesnakes can also be seen—and heard.

Kansas also has many birds. Kansas schoolchildren voted the western meadowlark the state bird. One famous Kansas "bird" is just make-believe. It is called the Jayhawk. It is supposed to have a red head and wear yellow shoes. Kansas people who hated slavery were sometimes called Jayhawkers. Today the University of Kansas sports teams are called the Jayhawkers.

After visiting Dodge City, head for northwest Kansas. At Colby, visit the Sod Town Pioneer Museum.

The pioneers had no traffic signs when they traveled. They knew where they were when they came to rivers or rock formations. Castle Rock and the Kansas Pyramids in northwest Kansas served as guideposts.

Right: The state bird of Kansas is the western meadowlark.
Below: Monument Rocks in northwest Kansas rise up to 60 feet high.

The Eisenhower Library and Museum in Abilene

Going northeast from Castle Rock you will come to the Pawnee Indian Village Museum. This is not far from the Nebraska border. There you can see Pawnee earthlodges. You can see how these people hunted, farmed, and lived. About 75 miles south, near Salina (sah • LINE • ah), is the Indian Burial Pit. Skeletons of ancient Indians have been found there.

Would you like to see the home of a president? To finish your trip, go a few miles east of Salina to the town of Abilene. There, visit the Eisenhower Library and Museum. You can see the house where Dwight David Eisenhower grew up.

Amelia Earhart's home

Many interesting people besides Dwight David Eisenhower have lived in the Sunflower State.

Amelia Earhart (1897-?) was born in Atchison. Amelia Earhart became the first woman to fly an airplane across the Atlantic Ocean. In 1937, she tried an around-the-world flight. She disappeared somewhere over the Pacific Ocean. Her airplane was never found, and neither was she. Most people think she crashed into the ocean.

Ronald E. Evans of St. Francis made it back from his big flight. Evans is an astronaut. In 1972 he was pilot of the *Apollo 17* command module. Evans flew around the moon while two other astronauts landed on it.

The governor's mansion in Topeka

Alfred M. Landon moved to Kansas as a young man. He was elected governor of Kansas twice. In 1936 he ran for president. That was one election Alf Landon lost.

In 1978 Alf Landon's daughter made history. Her name is Nancy Landon Kassebaum. In November of 1978 she was elected senator of Kansas. There have been other women senators. But the others followed their husbands as senator. Nancy Landon Kassebaum is the first American woman elected senator on her own for a full term.

Kansas wheat being loaded onto a barge.

One of Kansas's most famous "people" is a storybook girl! Her name is Dorothy, and she is the girl in *The Wizard of Oz*. "There's no place like home!" most Kansans feel, just as Dorothy did.

Home to Pawnee Indians ... President Eisenhower ... and Amelia Earhart.

Vast plains where buffalo once roamed.

"Cow towns" like Dodge City and Abilene where Wyatt Earp and "Wild Bill" Hickok once lived.

The leading wheat-growing state ... the leading state for making small airplanes ... and a leading cattle state.

This is the Sunflower State—Kansas.

Facts About KANSAS

Area—82,277 square miles (14th biggest state)

Greatest Distance North to South—204 miles

Greatest Distance East to West—411 miles

Border States—Nebraska on the north; Missouri on the east; Oklahoma on the south; Colorado on the west

Highest Point—4,039 feet above sea level (Mount Sunflower)

Lowest Point—680 feet above sea level (along Verdigris River)

Hottest Recorded Temperature—121° (at Fredonia on July 18, 1936, and also near Alton on July 24, 1936)

Coldest Recorded Temperature—Minus 40° (at Lebanon on February 13, 1905)

Statehood—Our 34th state, on January 29, 1861

Origin of Name Kansas—Named for the Kansa Indians; Kansa means "people of the south wind"

Capital—Topeka (1861)

Previous Capitals—Fort Leavenworth, Shawnee Mission, Pawnee, and Lecompton served as capitals while Kansas was a territory

Counties—105

U.S. Senators—2

U.S. Representatives—5

Electoral Votes—7

State Senators—40

State Representatives—125

State Song—"Home on the Range"; words written by Dr. Brewster M. Higley, music by Daniel Kelley

State Marching Song—"The Kansas March" by Duff E. Middleton

State Motto—*Ad Astra per Aspera* (Latin meaning "To the Stars Through Difficulties")

Nicknames—Sunflower State; Breadbasket of America; Jayhawker State; Wheat State; Midway, U.S.A.

State Seal—Adopted in 1861

State Flag—Adopted in 1927 (word "KANSAS" added in 1961)

State Flower—Sunflower

State Bird—Western meadowlark (chosen by Kansas schoolchildren)

State Animal—Buffalo

State Insect—Honey bee (chosen by Kansas schoolchildren)

State Tree—Cottonwood

Some Colleges and Universities—Baker University, Bethany College, Fort Hays State University, University of Kansas, Kansas State University of Agriculture and Applied Science, Marymount College, Washburn University of Topeka, Wichita State University

Main Rivers—Kansas and Arkansas

Some Other Rivers—Republican, Smoky Hill, Neosho, Cimarron, Big Blue, Verdigris, Saline, Solomon, Missouri

Lakes—About 150 (most of them are man-made and used for irrigation and drinking water; the biggest lake in the state is Tuttle Creek Reservoir)

State Parks—23

Animals—Deer, rabbits, prairie dogs, coyotes, raccoons, opossums, squirrels, beavers, bobcats, mink, badgers, muskrats, skunks, foxes, buffalo, prairie chickens, quail, doves, pheasants, ducks, rattlesnakes, copperheads, cottonmouths (water moccasins)

Fishing—Bass, crappie, catfish, bluegills, perch, pike

Farm Products—Wheat, beef cattle, corn, hogs, sorghum grain, alfalfa hay, milk, soybeans, oats, barley, sugar beets, alfalfa seeds, sheep

Mining—Oil, natural gas, helium, salt, coal

Manufacturing Products—Airplanes, railroad cars, other transportation equipment, farm machines and other machinery, flour, meat products, other food products, chemicals, oil products, rubber products, glass products, soap, cement

Population—1980 census: 2,364,236 (1985 estimate: 2,450,000)

Major Cities	1980 Census	1984 Estimate
Wichita	279,835	283,500
Kansas City	161,148	160,500
Topeka	115,266	118,900
Overland Park	81,784	
Lawrence	52,738	54,200
Hutchinson	40,284	
Salina	41,843	

44

Kansas History

The earliest people in Kansas lived there at least 10,000 years ago. People may have been in Kansas over 20,000 years ago.

About 1000 A.D.—Early Indians learn to garden; this is the first farming in Kansas

1541—Spaniard Coronado, looking for gold, crosses Arkansas River near present-day Dodge City; Spain claims area

1542—Father Juan de Padilla, a Spanish missionary with Coronado, returns to Kansas but is killed by Indians

1601—Spaniard Juan de Oñate explores Kansas

1682—France claims large area, including Kansas

1719—Frenchman Charles Claude de Tisné explores and visits with Osage Indians

1724—French explorer Bourgmont enters Kansas

1762—Area comes under control of Spain, but French fur traders remain

1800—France regains control

1803—By Louisiana Purchase, Kansas becomes part of the United States

1804—American explorers Lewis and Clark camp in Kansas

1806—Zebulon M. Pike explores Kansas for United States

1821—Santa Fe Trail, going through Kansas, is established

1825—Osage and Kansa Indians give up some of their lands

1827—Fort Leavenworth is built as an army post to protect people traveling through Kansas

1842—By now, many tribes have been moved to reservations in "Indian Country" of Kansas

1843—Wyandot Indians found town of Wyandotte which becomes Kansas City

1849—Because of California gold rush, 90,000 people pass through Kansas on their way out West

1850s—People fight over slavery in "Bleeding Kansas"; at least 55 are killed

1854—Territory of Kansas is established

1856—Slave State people burn part of Lawrence; then at Pottawatomie Creek John Brown kills five Slave State men

1859—Kansas bans slavery

1860—Population is 107,206

1861—On January 29th, Kansas becomes our 34th state; Topeka is the capital

1861-1865—During Civil War, Kansas sends 20,149 men to fight in Union (Northern) Army

1863—At Lawrence, Quantrill and his raiders kill 150 people on August 21

1864—Confederate (Southern) troops beaten at Mine Creek in only Civil War battle inside Kansas

1867—Big Indian attacks; then Medicine Lodge Peace Treaty is signed, with Indians losing much land

1870—Wichita founded

1874—Great Grasshopper Plague destroys crops; in this same year the Russian Mennonites bring Turkey Red wheat to Kansas

1878—End of Indian fighting

1878-1880—During this time, about 40,000 blacks from former slave states arrive in Kansas

1880—Dodge City is biggest cattle market in the world

1885—End of cattle drives from Texas

1887—Susanna Medora Salter of Argonia becomes first woman mayor in United States

1892—Oil is found near Neodesha

1900—Population of state is 1,470,495; Carry Nation begins smashing saloons

1903—State Capitol Building is completed in Topeka

1903—First helium find in United States, near Dexter

1912—Women gain right to vote in Kansas

1914-1918—During World War I, 80,261 Kansans fight for U.S.

1915-1919—Jess Willard of Emmett is world's heavyweight boxing champion

1928—Charles Curtis of Kansas is elected vice-president

1934-1936—Dust storms and droughts hit Kansas

1936—Alf Landon runs for president but loses to Franklin D. Roosevelt

1939-1945—During World War II, 215,000 Kansas men and women are in uniform

1952—Dwight D. Eisenhower of Abilene is elected 34th president

1952-1957—Very dry weather in Kansas, but the state now has irrigation projects to bring water to crops

1954—U.S. Supreme Court rules in *Brown versus the Board of Education of Topeka* that segregated schools break the law

1961—Happy 100th birthday, Sunflower State!

1966—Topeka hit by huge tornado that kills 16 and injures over 400

1972—Governor's term increased from two to four years

1978—Nancy Landon Kassebaum is first woman elected to the U.S. Senate for a full term on her own

1987—Mike Hayden begins first term as governor.

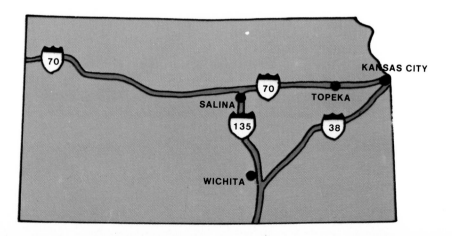

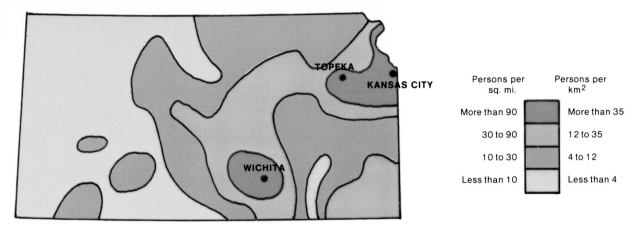

Persons per sq. mi.		Persons per km²
More than 90		More than 35
30 to 90		12 to 35
10 to 30		4 to 12
Less than 10		Less than 4

INDEX

47

About the Author:

Dennis Fradin attended Northwestern University on a creative writing scholarship and graduated in 1967. While still at Northwestern, he published his first stories in *Ingenue* magazine and also won a prize in *Seventeen's* short story competition. A prolific writer, Dennis Fradin has been regularly publishing stories in such diverse places as *The Saturday Evening Post, Scholastic, National Humane Review, Midwest,* and *The Teaching Paper.* He has also scripted several educational films. Since 1970 he has taught second grade reading in a Chicago school—a rewarding job, which, the author says, "provides a captive audience on whom I test my children's stories." Married and the father of three children, Dennis Fradin spends his free time with his family or playing a myriad of sports and games with his childhood chums.

About the Artists:

Len Meents studied painting and drawing at Southern Illinois University and after graduation in 1969 he moved to Chicago. Mr. Meents works full time as a painter and illustrator. He and his wife and child currently make their home in LaGrange, Illinois.

Richard Wahl, graduate of the Art Center College of Design in Los Angeles, has illustrated a number of magazine articles and booklets. He is a skilled artist and photographer who advocates realistic interpretations of his subjects. He lives with his wife and two sons in Libertyville, Illinois.